Diabetic Cookbook

On a Budget

Pork & Lamb Recipes

Great-tasting, Easy and Healthy Recipes for Every Day

Angela Moore

2

Table of Contents

4

Intruduction

If you have diabetes, watching what you eat is by far one of the most important ways of staying healthy. The goal should be to avoid spikes in your blood sugar (blood glucose levels). Some people interpret this as needing to completely avoid sugar and carbohydrates, which isn't entirely accurate. In fact, people typically need 40-60% of their calories to come from carbohydrates. It's the amount and consistency of carbohydrates in a diabetic diet that makes the biggest difference in controlling blood glucose levels.

As a diabetic, you can and should eat a wide variety of foods. So instead of focusing on eliminating certain foods from your diet, emphasize increasing vegetables and fruits, limiting added fats and sugars, and paying close attention to portion size. For example, it's probably okay to eat peaches, melons, and dried fruits if you are being carefully not to eat too much. These basic healthy eating practices are key, along with establishing a regular exercise routine. Establishing lasting healthy behaviors is much more important than focusing on how much weight you need to lose right now, and the foods you should eliminate from your diet.

What does the diet consist of?

The diabetic diet can vary from person to person depending on diagnosis, current nutritional status, blood glucose levels, glycated haemoglobin, blood lipids, and blood pressure. Regardless, it generally consists of monitoring the daily intake of macronutrients: carbohydrates, protein, and fat. Specifically, patients need to watch their carbohydrate intake because it is the main factor affecting postprandial blood glucose levels.

What are the nutritional recommendations of a diabetic diet?

The amount of carbohydrate in the diet is individualized based on the person's usual intake and desired glucose and lipid goals. Daily intake of carbohydrates can range from 45% to 60% of total calories. Blood glucose and insulin response are influenced by both the source and amount of carbohydrates consumed. Of the two, priority is given to the total amount of carbohydrate consumed at each meal and snack rather than the source of carbohydrate.

Protein intake should consist of 10% to 20% of the daily calories. Dietary protein can be obtained from vegetable and animal sources. Fat intake should be 25% to 30% of total calories for the day. It is important to keep track of your lipid levels with your doctor. Cholesterol should be limited to less than 300 mg a day.

1. Festive Pork

Serves 4.

Ingredients:

- 1 (3/4 lb.) pork tenderloin, trimmed
- 1 tablespoon olive or vegetable oil
- 1/2 cup low–sodium beef broth, divided
- 2 tablespoons dried cranberries
- 1 1/2 teaspoons Dijon mustard
- 1 tablespoon orange juice concentrate
- 1 teaspoon cornstarch

Directions:

1. Cut tenderloin into 12 slices; flatten to 1/4–inch thickness.
2. Brown in oil in a skillet over medium heat. Add 1/4 cup of the beef broth;
3. Cover and simmer for 5 to 10 minutes or until meat is no longer pink.
4. Remove meat to a serving dish and keep warm.
5. Add cranberries, mustard and remaining broth to the skillet.
6. Combine orange juice concentrate and cornstarch until smooth;
7. Gradually add to broth mixture, stirring constantly. Bring to a boil;
8. Cook and stir for 1 to 2 minutes. Pour over pork.

Nutritional Analysis: One serving equals 162 calories,

92 mg sodium, 50 mg cholesterol, 5 gm carbohydrate, 19 gm protein, 7 gm fat

2. Oven–Fried Pork Chops

Serves 4

Ingredients:

- 1 1/2 C. non–fat dry milk
- 1 T. paprika
- 2 Teaspoon. poultry seasoning
- 1/4 Teaspoon. pepper
- 4 (1 pound) pork chops

Directions:

1. Combine first four ingredients in a large resealable plastic bag.
2. Add pork, one piece at a time, and shake to coat.
3. Place in an 8-inch square baking pan that has been coated with non-stick cooking spray.
4. Bake, uncovered, at 350°F for 30 minutes or until juices run clear.
5. Bake for 1 hour or until meat thermometer reads 160°F to 170°F.

Nutritional Analysis: 240 calories, 204 mg sodium, 78 mg cholesterol, 15 gm carbohydrate, 36 gm protein, 4 gm fat.

3. Memphis Spare Ribs

Yield: 4 servings

Ingredients:

- 2 pounds (900 g) pork spareribs
- 1/4 cup (60 ml) cider vinegar

Rub

- 1/2 cup (115 g) brown sugar
- 11/2 teaspoons black pepper
- 1 teaspoon cayenne pepper

Sauce

- 8 ounces (225 g) no-salt-added tomato sauce
- 1/2 cup (120 ml) cider vinegar
- 1/4 cup (85 g) honey
- 1 teaspoon onion powder
- 1 teaspoon dry mustard
- 1 teaspoon garlic powder
- 1/2 teaspoon cayenne pepper

Directions:

1. Brush ribs with vinegar.
2. Mix rub ingredients together and rub into ribs.
3. Smoke or grill until done.
4. While ribs are cooking, combine sauce ingredients.
5. Brush with sauce during the last 30 minutes of cooking.

Nutritional Info: 162 g water; 529 calories (45% from fat, 15% from protein, 39% from carb); 21 g protein; 27 9 total fat; 10 g

4.Pineapple-Stuffed Pork Chops

Yeld: 4 Serving

Ingredients:

- 4 pork loin chops, 1-inch (21/2 cm) thick
- 8 ounces (225 g) pineapple slices
- 1/4 cup (60 g) low-sodium ketchup
- 1 tablespoon (6 g) chopped green onion
- 1/2 teaspoon dry mustard

Directions:

1. Cut a pocket in each chop to make room for pineapple.
2. Drain pineapple, reserving liquid.

3. Cut two slices in half; cut up remaining pineapple and set aside.
4. Place a half pineapple slice in the pocket of each chop.
5. Heat grill to medium and grill about 20 minutes, turning once.
6. Meanwhile, in a small saucepan combine ketchup, green onion, mustard, and the reserved pineapple juice and pieces.
7. Heat to boiling, reduce heat, and simmer 10 minutes.
8. Grill chops 5 minutes more, brushing with sauce and turning several times.

Nutritional Info: 131 g water; 189 calories (21 % from fat, 46% from protein, 33% from carb); 22 g protein; 4 g total fat;

5. Sweet and Sour Skillet Pork Chops

Yeld: 6 Serving

Ingredients:

- 6 pork chops
- 6 pineapple rings, juice packed
- 1/2 cup (120 ml) pineapple juice
- 2 tablespoons (30 ml) cider vinegar
- 1/4 tablespoon brown sugar substitute, such as Splenda
- 1/4 teaspoon cinnamon
- Dash rosemary
- 1 cup (100 g) celery, cut into strips
- 1 cup (150 g) green bell pepper, cut into strips

Directions:

1. Trim all fat from chops.
2. Brown meat on both sides in skillet sprayed with nonstick vegetable oil spray.
3. Remove chops. In skillet, mix pineapple juice, vinegar, and sugar substitute.
4. Add cinnamon and rosemary.
5. Put chops in pan. Add celery and cover.

6. Simmer about 30 minutes. Add green pepper strips. Place pineapple rings on each chop.
7. Cover and cook about 10 minutes longer.
8. Arrange chops on serving platter.
9. Place pineapple and pepper strips on top. Spoon juice over top.

Nutritional Info: 98 g water; 274 calories (50% from fat, 35% from protein, 15% from carb); 24 g Protein; 15 9 total fat; 5 g

6.Barbecued Pork Chops

Yeld: 4 Serving

Ingredients:

4 pork loin chops

6 tablespoons (90 ml) Dick's Reduced-Sodium Soy Sauce (see chapter 2)

1/2 teaspoon garlic powder

2 teaspoons (10 ml) sherry

1/2 cup (60 g) no-salt-added tomato sauce

1/4 cup (60 ml) water

Directions:

1. Trim fat away.
2. Mix soy sauce, garlic, sherry, and tomato sauce.
3. Pour over meat in flat pan.
4. Let stand, covered, in refrigerator for 3 hours.
5. Drain off marinade and pour into small pan.
6. Add water and heat to boiling.
7. Reduce heat and simmer 5 minutes.
8. Grill over medium heat until done, turning once. Serve hot sauce with meat.

Nutritional Info: 135 g water; 158 calories (26% from fat, 61 % from protein, 13% from carb); 23 g Protein; 4 g total fat; 1 g

7. Slow Cooker Pork Chops

Yeld: 4 Serving

Ingredients:

- 4 pork loin chops
- 1 cup (160 g) onion, sliced
- 1 tablespoon (1 5 g) brown sugar
- 1/4 cup (60 g) low-sodium catsup
- 1 tablespoon (15 ml) lemon juice
- 1/4 cup (60 ml) water

Directions:

1. Cut fat from chops.
2. In a slow cooker, layer pork chops, onion, brown sugar, catsup and lemon juice.
3. Pour water over all. Cook on low 8-10 hours.

Nutritional Info: 139 g water; 174 calories (23% from fat, 51 % from protein, 26% from carb); 22 g Protein; 4 gtotal fat; 1 g

8.   Zucchini Stuffed Pork Chops

Yeld: 4 Serving

Ingredients:

- 11/2 cup (188 g) zucchini, shredded
- 1 clove garlic, crushed
- 2 tablespoons (10 g) parmesan cheese, grated
- 1/4 teaspoon black pepper
- 4 boneless pork loin chops
- 1 teaspoon (5 ml) olive oil
- 1/2 cup (120 ml) dry white wine or chicken broth

- 1 tablespoon (11 g) Dijon mustard

Directions:

1. Squeeze zucchini with paper towels to remove moisture.
2. Spray 10-inch (25 cm) nonstick skillet with nonstick cooking spray.
3. Cook zucchini and garlic in skillet over medium heat about 3 minutes or until tender. Stir in cheese and pepper.
4. Remove zucchini mixture from skillet; cool.
5. Trim fat from pork chops.
6. Flatten each pork chop to 1/4-inch (5 mm) thickness between waxed paper or plastic wrap.
7. Spread one-fourth of the zucchini mixture over each piece of pork.
8. Roll up; secure with wooden picks.
9. Add oil and pork rolls to skillet. Cover and cook over medium heat 15 to 20 minutes, turning once, until done.
10. Remove wooden picks. Remove pork rolls from skillet; keep warm.
11. Add wine to skillet.
12. Cook over high heat 2 to 3 minutes or until reduced by half. Stir in mustard. Pour sauce over pork rolls.

Nutritional Info: 148 g water; 187 calories (36% from fat, 57% from protein, 7% from carb); 23 g Protein; 7 9 total fat; 2 g

9.Pork Chops in Onion Sauce

Yeld: 4 Serving

Ingredients:

- 4 pork loin chops
- 1/4 teaspoon pepper
- 11/2 tablespoons (12 g) flour
- 11/2 tablespoons (25 ml) olive oil
- 4 small onions, thinly sliced
- 1/2 cup (120 ml) beer
- 1/2 cup (120 ml) low-sodium beef broth
- 1 teaspoon cornstarch

Directions:

1. Season pork chops with pepper; coat with flour.
2. Heat oil in a heavy skillet.
3. Add pork chops; fry for 3 minutes on each side. Add onions; cook for another 5 minutes, turning chops once.
4. Pour in beer and beef broth; cover and simmer 15 minutes.
5. Remove pork shops to a preheated platter.
6. Blend cornstarch with a small amount of cold water.
7. Stir into sauce and cook until thick and bubbly.
8. Pour over pork chops.

Nutritional Info: 238 g water; 250 calories (36% from fat, 39% from protein, 25% from carb); 23 g Protein; 10 g total fat; 2 g

10. Ham and Artichoke Hearts Scalloped Potatoes

Serves 4

Ingredients:

- 2 cups frozen artichoke hearts
- Nonstick spray
- 1 cup chopped onion
- 4 small potatoes, thinly sliced
- Sea salt and freshly ground black pepper to taste (optional)

- 1 tablespoon lemon juice
- 1 tablespoon dry white wine
- 1 cup Mock Cream (see recipe in Chapter 6)
- ½ cup nonfat cottage cheese
- 1 teaspoon dried parsley
- 1 teaspoon garlic powder
- ½cup freshly grated Parmesan cheese
- ½ pound (4 ounces) cubed lean ham
- 2 ounces grated Cheddar cheese (to yield ½ cup)

Directions:

1. Preheat oven to 300°F.

2. Thaw artichoke hearts and pat dry with a paper towel. In deep casserole dish treated with nonstick spray, layer artichokes, onion, and potatoes; lightly sprinkle salt and pepper over top (if using).

3. In a food processor or blender, combine lemon juice, wine, Mock Cream, cottage cheese, parsley, garlic powder, and Parmesan cheese; process until smooth. Pour over

layered vegetables; top with ham. Cover casserole dish (with a lid or foil); bake 35– 40 minutes or until potatoes are cooked through.

4. Remove cover; top with Cheddar cheese. Return to oven another 10 minutes or until cheese is melted and bubbly. Let rest 10 minutes before cutting.

Nutritional Analysis (per serving, without salt):

Calories: 269 Protein: 21g Carbohydrates: 31g Fat: 8g Saturated Fat: 4g Cholesterol: 28mg Sodium: 762mg Fiber: 6g

11.   Italian Sausage

Yields about 2 pounds

Ingredients:

- 2 pounds (32 ounces) pork shoulder
- 1 teaspoon ground black pepper
- 1 teaspoon dried parsley
- 1 teaspoon Italian-style seasoning
- 1 teaspoon garlic powder
- 3/4 teaspoon crushed anise seeds
- 1/8 teaspoon red pepper flakes
- ½ teaspoon paprika
- ½ teaspoon instant minced onion flakes
- 1 teaspoon kosher or sea salt (optional)

Directions:

1. Remove all fat from meat; cut the meat into cubes. Put in food processor; grind to desired consistency.

2. Add remaining ingredients; mix until well blended. You can put sausage mixture in casings, but it works equally well broiled or grilled as patties.

Nutritional Analysis (per serving, without salt):

Calories: 135 Protein: 15g Carbohydrates: 0g Fat: 8g Saturated Fat: 3g Cholesterol: 45mg Sodium: 27mg Fiber: 0g

12. Italian Sweet Fennel Sausage

Yields about 2 pounds

Ingredients:

- 1 tablespoon fennel seeds
- ¼ teaspoon ground cayenne pepper
- 2 pounds (32 ounces) pork butt

- ½ teaspoon black pepper
- 2 ½ teaspoons crushed garlic
- 1 tablespoon sugar

Directions:

1. Toast fennel seeds and cayenne pepper in nonstick skillet over medium heat, stirring constantly, until seeds just begin to darken, about 2 minutes. Set aside.

2. Remove all fat from meat; cut the meat into cubes. Put in food processor; grind to desired consistency.

3. Add fennel and cayenne mixture plus remaining ingredients; mix until well blended.

4. You can put sausage mixture in casings, but it works equally well broiled or grilled as patties.

Nutritional Analysis (per serving, without salt):

Calories: 139 Protein: 15g Carbohydrates: 1g Fat: 8g Saturated Fat: 3g Cholesterol: 45mg Sodium: 27mg Fiber: 0g

13. Mock Chorizo

Yields about 2 pounds

Ingredients:

- 2 pounds (32 ounces) lean pork
- 4 tablespoons chili powder
- ¼ teaspoon ground cloves
- 2 tablespoons paprika
- 2 ½ teaspoons crushed fresh garlic
- 1 teaspoon crushed dried oregano
- 3 ½ tablespoons cider vinegar
- 1 teaspoon kosher or sea salt (optional)

Directions:

1. Remove all fat from meat; cut the meat into cubes. Put in food processor; grind to desired consistency.

2. Add remaining ingredients; mix until well blended.

3. Tradition calls for aging this sausage in an airtight container in the refrigerator for 4 days before cooking.

4. Leftover sausage can be stored in the freezer up to 3 months

Nutritional Analysis (per serving, without salt):

Calories: 137 Protein: 15g Carbohydrates: 1g Fat: 8g Saturated Fat: 3g

Cholesterol: 45mg Sodium: 27mg Fiber: 0g

14. Pork Chops with Mustard Cream Sauce

Yields: 4 serving

Ingredients:

- 1 pork chop, 1 inch thick
- 1 tablespoon olive oil
- 1 tablespoon dry white wine
- 1 tablespoon heavy cream
- 1 tablespoon spicy brown mustard or Dijon mustard
- Salt and Pepper

Directions:

1. Salt and pepper the chop on both sides.

2. Heat the oil in a heavy skillet over medium heat.

3. Saute the chop until they're browned on both sides and done through

4. Put the chop on a serving platter, and keep it warm.

5. Put the wine in the skillet, and stir it around, scraping all the tasty brown bits off the pan as you stir.

6. Stir in the cream and mustard, blend well, and cook for a minute or two. Pour over the chop and serve.

15.   Pork Chops with Garlic and Balsamic Vinegar

Yields: 4 serving

Ingredients:

- 2 tablespoons olive oil
- 2 or 3 pork rib chops, 2 inches thick
- 3 tablespoons balsamic vinegar
- 3 cloves garlic, crushed
- 1/4 teaspoon guar or xanthan

Directions:

1. Put the oil in a large, heavy skillet over medium-high heat, and sear the chops in the oil until well-browned on both sides. Add the vinegar and garlic.

2. Cover the skillet, turn the burner to low, and let the chops simmer for 1 hour.

3. Remove the chops to a serving platter or serving plates, and put the liquid from the pan into a blender.

4. Add the guar or xanthan, run the blender for a few moments, and pour the thickened sauce over the chops.

16.   Pork Chili

Yields: 4 serving

Ingredients:

- 3/4 cup (120 g) chopped onion
- 4 cloves garlic, crushed
- 2 tablespoons (30 ml) olive oil

- 1 1/2 pounds (680 g) boneless pork loin, cut in 1/2" (1.25 cm) cubes
- 2 1/2 teaspoons chili powder
- 1 teaspoon ground cumin
- 1 green pepper, chopped
- 1 cup (240 ml) chicken broth
- 1/4 cup (60 g) chili sauce
- 3 chipotle chiles canned in adobo, minced
- Salt

Directions:

1. In your big heavy skillet, or better yet, in a Dutch oven, saute the onion and garlic in the olive oil until the onions are translucent.
2. Add everything else except the ground pumpkin seeds and the salt, turn the burner to low, cover the pan, and let the whole thing simmer for 45 minutes to an hour.
3. Salt to taste, and serve.

17.   Ham'n'Eggs

Yields: 4 serving

Ingredients:

- 1/2 head cauliflower
- 3 tablespoons (45 g) butter
- 1 tablespoon (7 g) curry powder
- 3 tablespoons (30 g) minced onion
- 2 cups (220 g) ham, cut in 1/2" (1.25 cm) cubes
- 4 hard-boiled eggs, coarsely chopped
- 1/4 cup (60 ml) heavy cream

- Salt and pepper
- 1/4 cup (15 g) chopped fresh parsley

Directions:

1. Run the cauliflower through the shredding blade of your food processor.
2. Put it in a microwaveable casserole with a lid, add a couple of tablespoons of water, cover, and microwave on high for 6 minutes.
3. Melt the butter in your large, heavy skillet over low heat, and add the curry powder and onion.
4. Sauté them together for 2 to 3 minutes.
5. Add everything else, stir gently but thoroughly, heat through, and serve.

18. Caribbean Jerk Pork Roast

Yields: 8 serving

Ingredients:

- 3 lbs pork loin, lean, boneless
- 1 Tablespoon onion flakes
- 1 Tablespoon onion powder
- 2 Teaspoon thyme
- 2 Teaspoon salt
- 1 Teaspoon ground allspice
- 1/2 Teaspoon ground nutmeg
- 1/2 Teaspoon ground cinnamon

- 2 Teaspoon splenda
- 1 Teaspoon black pepper
- 1 Teaspoon cayenne pepper

Directions:

Directions

1. Pat roast dry with paper toweling.
2. Blend seasonings and rub evenly over pork roast.
3. Place in shallow pan and roast at 350°F- 180°C for 45-60 minutes, until internal temperature registers 155°F-75°F.
4. Remove from oven, let rest 10 minutes
5. Slice and serve. Wrap leftovers well and refrigerate for tomorrow's sandwiches.

Nutritional Facts

396 Calories 28g Fat (65.5% calories from fat) 31g Protein 2g Carbohydrate

19. Perfectly High Performance Pork Chops

Yields: 4 serving

Ingredients:

- 4 pork chops (5 ounces each), ½ inch thick
- 1 medium sized white onion, chopped
- 1 large green bell pepper, chopped
- 1 large red bell pepper, chopped
- 1 small (6 ounce) can V-8®
- ½ t. canola oil

Directions

1. Spread canola oil on bottom of heavy skillet and heat over medium heat.
2. Place pork chops in skillet and brown the chops on both sides, (or about 15 minutes on each side).
3. Remove chops and keep warm.
4. Add the chopped onion and pepper, and sauté until crisp-tender, stirring constantly.
5. Add the V-8 to the vegetable mixture, and bring to a boil. Return the chops to the pan.
6. Reduce heat and simmer for an additional 12 to 15 minutes until the chops are tender.

7. Remove chops to a serving dish.

8. Spoon vegetable sauce over each chop. Serve immediately.

Nutritional Facts

Calories: 243 Carbohydrates: 7g Fiber: 2g Protein: 28g Fat: 10 g Saturated Fats: 3g Sodium: 269mg

20. Pork with Garlic Cream Sauce

Yields: 4 serving

Ingredients:

- 1 pound pork tenderloin
- 2 teaspoons canola oil
- 2 teaspoons sesame seeds, toasted, divided
- 1 to 2 garlic cloves, minced
- 1 tablespoon butter or stick margarine
- 1/3 cup 1% milk
- 3 oz reduced-fat cream cheese, cubed

- 1 tablespoon minced chives

Directions

1. Cut pork into 1" slices; flatten to 1/2" thickness. Place in a 15"x10"x1" baking dish coated with nonstick cooking spray.
2. Brush oil over all sides of pork; sprinkle with half of the sesame seeds. Broil 4-6" from the heat for 3-5 minutes longer or until meat juices run clear.
3. Meanwhile, in a saucepan, sauté garlic in butter for 1 minute. Stir in milk and cream cheese.
4. Reduce heat; cook and stir until blended and smooth. Stir in chives. Serve with pork.

Nutritional Facts

Calories: 255 Fat: 14 g (6 g sat) Cholesterol: 88mg Sodium: 151 mg Carbohydrates: 3 g Fiber: trace Protein: 27 g Diabetic Exchanges: 4 lean meat, 1 fat Servings: 4

21.   Mediterranean Pork Chops

Yields: 4 serving

Ingredients:

- 4 boneless or bone-in pork loin chops, cut 1/2 " thick(1 to 1 1/2 lbs)
- 1/2 teaspoon kosher salt

- 1/4 teaspoon freshly ground black pepper
- 1 tablespoon finely chopped fresh rosemary or 1 teaspoon dried rosemary, crushed
- 2 cloves garlic, minced

Directions

1. Sprinkle chops with kosher salt and pepper; set aside.
2. In a small bowl combine rosemary and garlic.
3. Sprinkle rosemary mixture evenly over both sides of each chop, rub in with your fingers.
4. Place chops on a rack in a shallow roasting pan.
5. Roast chops in a 425 degrees oven for 10 minutes.
6. Reduce heat to 350 degrees and continue roasting about 25 minutes or until pork chop registers 160 degree F.

Nutritional Facts

Calories: 147 Fat: 4 g (Sat: 2 g) Cholesterol: 71 mg Sodium: 288 mg

Carbohydrates: 1 g Fiber: 24 g

22.   Japanese Crockpot Lamb

Yields: 8 serving

Ingredients:

- 2 lb Lamb
- 1/4 cup soy sauce
- 1 Tablespoon Honey
- 2 Tablespoon Vinegar
- 2 Tablespoon Sherry
- 2 Garlic clove -- crushed
- 1/4 Teaspoon Ginger -- ground
- 1 1/2 cups chicken stock -- optional

Directions

1. Put all ingredients in crockpot and cook all day on LOW.

Nutritional Facts

257 Calories 19g Fat (68.7% calories from fat) 15g Protein 4g Carbohydrate

23. Squash Stuffed with Lamb and Rice

Serves 4; Serving Size: 1 stuffed squash

Ingredients:

- 3 cups chopped tomatoes
- 1 cup chopped onion
- 2 cups water
- ½ teaspoon salt
- ¼ teaspoon freshly ground pepper, divided
- 2 tablespoons minced fresh mint
- 4 small zucchini squash (7"–8" long)
- ¾ pound very lean ground lamb
- ½ cup rice

- 2 tablespoons pine nuts
- ½ teaspoon salt
- 1/8 teaspoon ground allspice

Directions:

1. Prepare tomato sauce first: Combine tomatoes, onion, water, salt,/teaspoon pepper, and fresh mint in a large pot. Bring to a boil; reduce heat and simmer 30 minutes.

2. Scrub squash and dry with paper towels. Remove stem ends of each squash and carefully core center, leaving about/" of shell.

3. Make stuffing: Thoroughly mix ground lamb, rice, pine nuts, salt, allspice, and remaining/teaspoon pepper.

4. Spoon stuffing into each squash, tapping bottom end of squash to get stuffing down. Fill each squash to top; stuffing should be loosely packed to allow rice to expand while cooking.

5. Place squash in tomato sauce, lying them on their sides. Bring sauce to a slow boil;

cover and cook over low heat for 45–60 minutes or until squash is tender and rice has cooked.

6. Serve squash with tomato sauce spooned over top.

Nutritional Analysis:

Calories: 430 Protein: 27g Carbohydrates: 36g Fat: 20g

Saturated Fat: 7g Cholesterol: 82mg Sodium: 692mg Fiber: 5g

24. Baked Stuffed Kibbeh

Serves 8;

Ingredients:

- Cooking spray
- ¾ cup fine-grind bulgur wheat
- 2 cups boiling water
- 1 pound lean ground lamb
- 1 cup grated onion, divided
- 1 teaspoon salt
- ¼ teaspoon pepper
- Small bowl ice water
- 3 tablespoons butter, divided
- ¼ cup pine nuts
- ¼ teaspoon ground cinnamon
- ¼ teaspoon ground allspice

Directions:

1. Preheat oven to 350°F. Spray 9" × 9" baking dish with cooking spray.

2. Put bulgur wheat in small bowl. Cover with boiling water and allow wheat to absorb liquid, approximately 15–20 minutes.

3. Line colander with small piece of cheesecloth. Drop bulgur wheat into cloth; drain and squeeze as much liquid out of wheat as possible.

4. On large cutting board, combine lamb,/cup grated onions, wheat, salt, and pepper; mix with hands, kneading together all ingredients.

5. Divide meat mixture in half. Place half in bottom of baking dish by dipping hands into ice water to spread meat mixture smoothly over bottom of dish. Cover bottom of dish completely.

6. In a small pan, melt 1/tablespoons of butter; sauté remaining/ cup onions, pine nuts, cinnamon, and allspice until onions are soft.

7. Spread onion and pine nut mixture evenly over first layer of meat in baking dish. Take remaining half of meat mixture and spread smoothly on top, using procedure in step 5.

8. Score top in diamond shapes with a knife dipped in cold water. Melt remaining 1 ½ tablespoons of butter; drizzle over top of meat. Bake for approximately 40–45 minutes or until gold brown.

Nutritional Analysis (per serving):

Calories: 226 Protein: 18g Carbohydrates: 13g Fat: 12g Saturated Fat: 4g Cholesterol: 62mg Sodium: 343mg Fiber: 3g

25. Pork Lo Mein

Serves 4;

Ingredients:

- 1 ½ tablespoons reduced-sodium soy sauce
- 1 teaspoon grated fresh ginger
- 1 tablespoon rice vinegar

- ¼ teaspoon ground turmeric
- ¾ -pound lean pork loin, cut into 1" cubes
- ½ tablespoon canola oil
- ½ cup sliced green onion
- 2 teaspoons minced garlic
- 2 cups shredded cabbage
- 1 cup (cut into 1" pieces) snap peas
- ¼ teaspoon crushed red pepper
- 2 cups cooked whole-grain spaghetti
- 1 teaspoon sesame oil
- 1 teaspoon sesame seeds

Directions:

1. Combine soy sauce, ginger, rice vinegar, and turmeric in bowl. Mix in cubed pork; set aside.

2. In large skillet or wok, heat oil and sauté onion and garlic. Add meat; cook quickly until meat and onions are slightly browned.

3. Add in cabbage and snap peas; continue to stir-fry for another 3–4 minutes. Sprinkle in crushed red pepper.

4. When vegetables are crisp-tender, add cooked pasta, sesame oil, and sesame seeds.Toss lightly and serve.

Nutritional Analysis (per serving):

Calories: 266 Protein: 23g Carbohydrates: 25g Fat: 8g

Saturated Fat: 2g Cholesterol: 50mg Sodium: 386mg Fiber: 5g

26. Lamb Shanks with White Beans and Carrots

Serves 4; Serving Size: 1 lamb shank

Ingredients:

- 4 lamb shanks, well-trimmed
- Salt and pepper to taste
- 1 tablespoon olive oil
- 1 large yellow onion, peeled and chopped
- 4 garlic cloves, minced
- 1 medium carrot, peeled and cut into chunks

- 2 tablespoons tomato paste
- 1 cup dry red wine
- 1 cup gluten-free chicken broth
- 2 bay leaves
- ½ cup chopped parsley
- 2 (13-ounce) cans white beans, drained and rinsed

Directions:

1. Sprinkle the lamb shanks with the salt and pepper.
2. In a large frying pan over medium-high heat, add the olive oil, lamb, onion, garlic, and carrot and cook until the lamb is browned, about 5 minutes.
3. Stir in the tomato paste, red wine, chicken broth, bay leaves, and parsley.
4. Cover the pot and simmer for 1 hour.
5. Add the white beans and simmer for another 30 minutes.
6. Remove the bay leaves before serving.

Nutritional Analysis (per serving):

Calories: 417 Protein: 31g Carbohydrates: 44g Fat: 12g Saturated Fat: 3g

Cholesterol: 75mg 1 4 Sodium: 601mg Fiber: 6g

27.   Lamb and Root Vegetable Tagine

Serves 6;

Ingredients:

- 2-pound leg of lamb, trimmed of fat and cut into bite-sized chunks
- 1 tablespoon olive oil
- ½ medium onion, peeled and chopped
- 1 clove garlic, minced
- ½ teaspoon ground black pepper
- ½ teaspoon salt
- 1 cup gluten-free chicken stock
- ½ pound (about 2 medium) sweet potatoes, peeled and cut into 1" chunks
- 1/3 cup dried apricots, cut in half
- 1 teaspoon ground coriander
- 1 teaspoon ground cumin
- ¼ teaspoon ground cinnamon

Directions:

1. In a large skillet, brown the cubed lamb in the olive oil over medium-high heat, approximately 1–2 minutes per side.

2. Add the lamb to a greased 4-quart slow cooker.

3. Cook the onion and garlic in the same skillet over medium-high heat for 3–4 minutes until soft and then add them to the slow cooker.

4. Add the remaining ingredients to the slow cooker.

5. Cook on high for 4 hours or on low for 8 hours.

Nutritional Analysis (per serving):

Calories: 270 Protein: 32g Carbohydrates: 14g Fat: 9g Saturated Fat: 2.5g Cholesterol: 100mg Sodium: 480mg Fiber: 2g

28. Grass-Fed Lamb Meatballs

Serves 6;

Ingredients:

- ¼ cup pine nuts
- 4 tablespoons olive oil, divided
- 1 ½ pounds ground grass-fed lamb

- ¼ cup minced garlic
- 2 tablespoons cumin

Directions:

1. Over medium-high heat in a medium frying pan, sauté the pine nuts in 2 tablespoons of olive oil for 2 minutes until brown. Remove them from the pan and allow them to cool.

2. In a large bowl, combine the lamb, garlic, cumin, and pine nuts and form the mixture into meatballs.

3. Add the remaining olive oil to the pan and fry the meatballs until cooked through, about 5–10 minutes depending on size of meatballs.

Nutritional Analysis (per serving):

Calories: 320 Protein: 24g Carbohydrates: 3g Fat: 21g Saturated Fat: 4.5g Cholesterol: 75mg Sodium: 75mg Fiber: 1g

29.   Crushed Herb Lamb

Yield: 8 servings

Ingredients:

- 1 leg of lamb (5 112 pounds or 2112 kg)
- 6 cloves garlic
- 2 shallots
- 2 tablespoons (9 g) dried thyme
- 2 tablespoons (6 g) dried rosemary
- 2 tablespoons (12 g) pepper, freshly ground
- 1/4 cup (60 ml) olive oil

Directions:

1. Trim and discard fat and any transparent membrane from the surface of the lamb.
2. Peel garlic and shallots and cut into 1/4-inch-thick (1/2 cm thick) slivers.
3. Pierce lamb allover with the tip of a small knife and insert garlic and shallots into cuts (Iamb will look like a porcupine).
4. Mix thyme, rosemary, pepper, and olive oil and pat the mixture all over the lamb.
5. Roast at 350°F (180°C, gas mark 4) or grill over indirect heat until internal temperature reaches 125°F (52°C) for

rare or 135°F (57°C) for medium rare, about 1 hour and 10 minutes to 1 hour and 30 minutes.

Nutritional Info: 180 g water; 871 calories (62% from fat, 38% from protein, 1 % from carb); 80 g protein; 58 9 total fat; 22 g

30. Lamb Stew

Yield: 4 servings

Ingredients:

- 1 tablespoon (15 ml) olive oil
- 2 cups (320 g) onion, thinly sliced
- 1 tablespoon (10 g) garlic, minced
- 1/4 cup (60 ml) red wine vinegar
- 2 pounds (900 g) lamb shoulder, trimmed and cut into 1-inch (2 112 cm) cubes
- 14 ounces (400 g) no-salt-added tomatoes
- 2 tablespoons (32 g) no-salt-added tomato paste

- 1 teaspoon basil
- 1 teaspoon oregano
- 2 bay leaves
- 1/4 teaspoon black pepper
- 1 cup (150 g) red bell pepper, sliced
- 1 cup (150 g) green bell pepper, sliced
- 1/3 cup (20 g) fresh parsley, finely minced

Directions:

1. In Dutch oven, heat oil.
2. Sauté onions and garlic until onions are soft, about 2 minutes.
3. Stir in vinegar and cook for 1 to 2 minutes over medium heat, scraping any browned bits from the bottom.
4. Add lamb, tomatoes, tomato paste, basil, oregano, bay leaves, salt and pepper to taste.
5. Stir well to blend. Bring to boil, reduce heat, cover, and cook until lamb is fork tender, about 1 to 11/2 hours.
6. Remove bay leaves; stir in the red and green peppers.
7. Cover and simmer over medium heat until peppers are crisp-tender, another 5 to 8 minutes.
8. Remove the bay leaves and stir in the parsley just before serving.

Nutritional Info: 404 g water; 534 calories (35% from fat, 51 % from protein, 14% from carb); 67 g Protein; 21 g total fat; 7 g

31.   Lamb and Vegetable Stew

Yield: 4 servings

Ingredients:

- 2 cups sliced mushrooms
- 1 large red bell pepper, diced
- 1 large carrot, cut into 1/2-inch-thick slices
- 1 unpeeled new potato, diced
- 1 parsnip, cut into 1/2-inch-thick slices
- 1 large leek, white part only, chopped
- 1 clove garlic, minced
- 1/2 cup reduced-sodium chicken broth
- 1/2 teaspoon dried thyme
- 1/4 teaspoon dried rosemary
- 1/8 teaspoon black pepper
- 12 ounces lamb shoulder meat, cut into 1-inch pieces
- 2 tablespoons all-purpose flour

Directions:

1. Place mushrooms, bell pepper, carrot, potato, parsnip, leek, and garlic in slow cooker.
2. Add chicken broth, thyme, rosemary and black pepper; stir.

3. Add lamb.

4. Cover; cook on LOW 6 to 7 hours.

5. Combine flour and 2 tablespoons liquid from slow cooker in small bowl. Stir flour mixture into slow cooker.

6. Cover; cook 10 minutes.

7. Stir in salt, if desired.

Nutrition Information:

Calories: 204 calories, Carbohydrates: 55 g, Protein: 21 g, Fat: 4 g, Saturated Fat: 1 g, Cholesterol: 82 mg, Sodium: 82 mg, Fiber: 3 g

32.   Lamb with Carrots

Serves:4

Ingredients

- 1 Tablespoon coconut oil
- 2 lb lamb shoulder chops
- 1 large onion (sliced)
- 1/2 c mushrooms (quartered)
- 3 clove garlic (sliced)
- 1/4 Teaspoon allspice
- 1 Teaspoon smoked paprika
- 3-5 sprig(s) of fresh thyme (or 3/4 teaspoon dried)

- 2-3 branches of fresh rosemary (or 1 teaspoon dried)
- 1/2 Teaspoon salt
- 2 bay leaves
- 1/2 Teaspoon freshly ground black pepper
- 1 c white wine
- 2 c chicken broth (no salt added)
- 1-2 c beef broth
- 8 medium carrots
- 1 Tablespoon Dijon mustard

Directions:

1. Preheat oven to 325 degrees F.
2. Lightly season your lamb with salt and pepper. In a large oven proof Dutch oven, heat the coconut oil over medium high heat Brown the lamb on each side for approx. 1-2 minutes.
3. Remove from the pot and set aside.
4. Add the onions, mushrooms, and garlic to the pot and cook for about 3 minutes until onions begin to soften.
5. Stir in allspice,paprika,salt & pepper,bay leaves and add the wine.
6. Then add the carrots and chicken broth. Bring to a boil and allow to cook for about 3 minutes.
7. Return meat to pot and lay on top of veggies and sauce.
8. Divide mustard and spread on top of each shoulder chop.

9. Top with thyme sprigs and rosemary.

10. Add enough beef broth to bring liquid to cover the sides of the lamb. Cover and place in oven for 2 hours.

11. Just let it cook undisturbed for 2 hours.

12. Remove meat and serve with veggies and broth.

13. Use the left overs (if there are any) for a great veggie and barley soup the next day or freeze it for another day

33. Braised Lamb with Garden-Vegetable

Yields: 4 Servings

Ingredients

- 2 ½ pounds boneless lamb leg, trimmed and cut into 2-inch cubes
- ½ teaspoon salt
- 1 tablespoon extra-virgin olive oil
- 1 medium carrot, finely chopped
- 1 small onion, finely chopped
- 1 tablespoon all-purpose flour
- 1 ¾ cups dry red wine
- 1 cup reduced-sodium beef broth
- Freshly ground pepper, to taste
- 4 cloves garlic, minced
- 1 tablespoon finely chopped fresh rosemary
- 1 14-ounce can diced tomatoes
- 1 cup pearl onions, peeled (see Tip), or frozen small onions, rinsed under warm water to thaw
- 1 cup baby turnips, peeled (1/4 inch of green left on) and halved, or regular turnips cut into 1/2-inch wedges
- 1 ½ cups baby carrots

- 1 1/2 cups peas, fresh or frozen
- 2 tablespoons chopped fresh parsley

Directions:

1. Season lamb with salt and pepper.
2. Heat oil in a large deep skillet or Dutch oven.
3. Add the lamb and cook, turning from time to time, until browned on all sides, about 6 minutes. Transfer to a plate.
4. Add carrot and onion to the pan; cook, stirring often, until lightly browned, about 3 minutes.
5. Sprinkle flour over the vegetables; stir to coat.
6. Add wine and scrape up any browned bits. Simmer until reduced slightly, 2 to 3 minutes.
7. Add broth, tomatoes, garlic and rosemary; bring to a simmer.
8. Return the lamb to the pan.
9. Reduce heat to low, cover and simmer for 1 1/4 hours, checking from time to time to make sure it does not boil too rapidly.
10. Stir in pearl onions, turnips and carrots.
11. Simmer, covered, until the lamb and vegetables are tender, about 30 minutes.
12. Add peas and heat through. Sprinkle with parsley and serve.

Nutrition Facts

Serving Size: About 1 1/3 Cups Per Serving: 420 calories; protein 43.2g; carbohydrates 16.4g; dietary fiber 4.1g; sugars 6.9g; fat 13.7g;

34. Lamb Burgers with Herbs

Yields: 6 servings

Ingredients:

- ¼ cup fresh parsley, chopped
- ½ tsp. Celtic sea salt
- 1 ½ pounds grass-fed ground lamb
- 2 cloves organic garlic, minced
- ¼ cup chopped organic red onion
- ½ tsp. freshly ground black pepper
- ½ tsp. dried organic oregano

Directions

1. In a medium bowl, knead the ground lamb with the onion, garlic, parsley, oregano and salt and pepper.
2. Shape the meat into patties about ½ inch thick, and transfer to a plate lined with plastic wrap.
3. Prepare grill or grill pan to medium-high.
4. Cook the burgers for 3-4 minutes per side if using grill/grill pan, or 6-8 minutes total in
5. Flavor wave, or until desired doneness.
6. Serve

Nutrition Info:

Calories 326 Sodium 263mg Potassium 283mg Protein 19g Cholesterol 83mg Sugar 0.32g Total Fat 27g

35. Roast Leg of Lamb

Ingredients

- 17oz lamb's leg
- 1 clove garlic
- 1 tbsp olive oil
- 1 pinch   salt
- ground pepper to taste [optional]
- ½ onions, coarsely chopped
- 1 sprig rosemary, fresh
- 1/4 cup   red wine

Directions:

1. Preheat the oven to 140°C/275°F.

2. Peel the garlic cloves and slice them in half lengthwise.

3. Cut small slits in the surface of the lamb with a sharp knife and put a piece of garlic into each slit.

4. Heat the oil in a casserole or roasting pan over medium heat. Brown the lamb thoroughly on each side until golden, about 7-8 min.

5. Add salt and pepper, then remove the lamb from the pan and set aside.

6. Coarsely chop the onion and sauté in the same pan, 4-5 min until translucent and soft. Put the lamb back into the pan, add the rosemary sprigs and wine.

7. Cover and cook in the middle of the oven.

8. Calculate 3 ½ h per kilo of meat.

9. When ready, the meat will fall apart when inserting a fork.

10. Serve.

Nutrition Info:

Calories 260 Fat13 g Saturated 3.5 g + Trans 0 g Cholesterol90 mg Sodium70 mg

36. Rosemary Lamb Chops

Yield: 4 servings

Ingredients

- 1 ½ teaspoons chopped fresh rosemary
- ½ teaspoon salt
- ¼ teaspoon freshly ground black pepper
- 1 garlic clove, minced
- 8 (3-ounce) lamb rib chops, trimmed
- 2 teaspoons olive oil

Directions:

1. Combine chopped rosemary, salt, pepper, and minced garlic in a small bowl.
2. Sprinkle herb mixture evenly over lamb; gently rub over lamb.
3. Heat a large skillet over medium-high heat.
4. Add oil to pan; swirl to coat.
5. Add lamb; cook 3 minutes on each side or until desired degree of doneness.
6. Remove lamb from pan; let stand 5 minutes.

Nutrition Facts

Per Serving: 157 calories; fat 9.7g; saturated fat 3g; mono fat 4.6g; poly fat 0.9g; protein 16g; carbohydrates 0.4g; fiber 0.1g; cholesterol 52mg; iron 1.4mg; sodium 344mg; calcium 12mg.

37. Lamb Shanks In Red Wine

Yield: 4 servings

Ingredients

- 4 lamb shanks
- 1 onion finely diced
- 1 bunch radish, cleaned and halved optional
- 2 stalks celery including leaves finely chopped
- 4 teaspoons garlic
- 2 tablespoons tomato paste

- 1 tablespoon Worcestershire sauce or 1 tablespoon Tamari
- 400 gm tin diced tomatoes sugar free
- 1 cup red wine
- 2 teaspoons mixed herbs
- 2 bay leaves
- Salt and pepper to taste
- 1-2 teaspoons Stevia Erythritol Blend I like to use this one

Directions:

1. Aside from the lamb shanks, mix all the ingredients together in the slow cooker pot.
2. Place the lamb shanks on top of the sauce and spoon additional sauce over the top of the lamb so it is well covered.
3. Slow cook for 7-8 hours or until cooked through and tender.
4. Tastes delicious served on Cauliflower Mash with a side serve of low carb vegetables such as green beans.
5. Simply carb this recipe up by serving with mashed potato.

Nutritional Information

Serving: 1shank | Calories: 516kcal | Carbohydrates: 6.4g | Protein: 34.3g | Fat: 31.6g | Fiber: 0.2g

38.   Lamb Shanks With Mash

Yield: 4 servings

Ingredients:

- 1/2 teaspoon olive oil (extra virgin)
- kg lamb shanks (lean French-trimmed lamb shanks, 4 x 350 grams)
- 2 large brown onions (finely chopped)
- 255 grams carrots (thickly sliced, 3 carrots)
- 170 grams celery ribs (finely chopped, 3 sticks)
- 125 ml white wine (1/2 cup)
- 1 can (810 grams) crushed tomatoes (Ardmona recommended)
- Fresh bay leaves (6 small)
- Lemon thyme (4 sprigs)
- 1 can (420 grams) garbanzo beans (no-added-salt chickpeas, rinsed and drained)
- Extra lemon thyme leaves, to serve

FOR MASHED POTATO

- 30 oz potatoes, unpeeled
- ½ cup low fat milk (warmed)
- White pepper, to season
-

Directions:

1. Preheat oven to 140C, fan forced.

2. Heat oil in a large non-stick frying pan over a medium-high heat and add lamb shanks and cook, turning often, for 6 to 7 minutes or until well browned and then transfer to a large ovenproof dish with a lid

3. Add onion, carrot and celery to frying pan and cook over a medium heat, stirring occasionally, for 5 to 7 minutes or until onion begins to soften and then increase heat to high and add the wine and cook stirring often, for 2 minutes and then add tomato and bring to a simmer.

4. Sprinkle bay leaves and thyme over lamb shanks and pour over tomato mixture or if using one pot return the lamb shanks to the tomato mixture and then cover and bake for 3 hours.

5. Add chickpeas and bake for a further 30 minutes or until lamb shanks are tender.

6. Meanwhile, to make mashed potato, put potatoes into a large saucepan cover with cold water.

7. Put lid on the pot and bring to the boil over a high heat and then reduce heat to medium and cook, partially covered, for 30 minutes or until potatoes are very tender.

8. Set aside for 10 minutes or until cool enough to peel.

9. Peel potatoes and return to pan and mash until almost smooth and then add milk and beat until smooth and season with pepper.
10. Divide mash between shallow serving bowls and top with a lamb shank and spoon over vegetable sauce and sprinkle with extra lemon thyme leaves and serve.

Nutritional info

Calories 1422.3 Total Fat - 95.6 g Saturated Fat - 41 g Cholesterol - 287.1 mg Sodium - 364.5 mg Total Carbohydrate - 65.7 g Dietary Fiber - 14.4 g Sugars - 17.4 g

39. Herb-Crusted Rack of Lamb

Yield: 4 Servings

Ingredients:

- 4 cloves garlic, minced
- 1/2 cup chopped fresh rosemary leaves
- 1/4 cup chopped fresh mint leaves
- salt to taste
- freshly ground black pepper
- 1 rack of New Zealand lamb, fully French trimmed
- 1/2 cup chopped fresh parsley leaves
- 1 cup plain bread crumbs
- 1 tablespoon Dijon mustard

Directions

1. In a small bowl, mix the garlic, salt, pepper, rosemary and mint together.
2. Rub the mixture over the lamb and refrigerate for an hour or overnight.
3. Meanwhile, combine the bread crumbs and parsley in a small bowl.
4. Season with salt and pepper and set aside.
5. Spray a roasting pan with nonstick spray and place it in the oven. Preheat the oven to 500F.

6. Place the lamb, meat-side down in the hot roasting pan and cook for 10 minutes. Remove the lamb from the oven and reduce the heat to 400F.

7. Turn the lamb meat-side up and brush the meat with the mustard. Spread the crumb mixture over the mustard and press it onto the meat.

8. Return to the oven and cook for 10 minutes more to brown the bread crumbs.

9. Let the meat rest for 5 minutes. Carve the racks into chops and serve.

Nutritional Information

Calories: 341 Fat: 12 grams Saturated Fat: 1 grams Fiber: 0.5 grams Sodium: 302 milligrams Cholesterol: 189 milligrams Protein: 35 grams Carbohydrates: 23 grams

40.   Slow Cooked Lamb Shank Curry

Yield: 4

Ingredients:

- 3 - 4 lamb shanks
- 2 cups unsweetened almond milk or coconut milk
- 2 cups lamb stock
- 2 medium red onions
- 3 cloves garlic
- 1 can (400g) chickpeas (drained & rinsed)

- 1/2 cup canola oil
- 2 Tbsp tomato paste
- 1 can (400g) diced tomatoes
- 3 Tbsp kashmira masala powder
- 1 Tbsp chilli powder (less if you don't like it too spicy)
- 1 Tbsp mustard powder
- 1 Tbsp coriander powder
- 1 Tbsp stevia
- 1 Tsp salt
- 1 Tsp cracked pepper

Directions:

1. Place a heavy based pot with a lid onto a high heat on the stove top
2. Dice the onion and grate the garlic
3. Once the pot is hot pour in the canola oil
4. Once the oil it hot too, place the lamb shanks in the pot and brown them, turning them so they get browned all over
5. Once brown, remove from the pot (place them on a plate or clean chopping board) and turn the heat down to medium
6. Place the onion and garlic in the pot and sauté until the onions are cooked and translucent
7. Add the masala, chili, mustard and coriander powder

8. Stir, combining the spices and cook for a minute or so until you smell the spices releasing the flavors

9. Place the shanks back into the pot and add the lamb stock, tomatoes, tomato paste, stevia, almond or coconut milk and chickpeas

10. Stir well to combine all of these ingredients

11. Remove the lid and simmer for approximately another 20 minutes - without the lid on the pot to reduce the sauce by about one-third (make sure you check regularly and stir again so it doesn't get stuck on the bottom)

12. Prepare your rice. I use brown basmati 2 minute rice. I find it's best for my sugar levels and the flavour matches nicely with the dish...Please don't use white rice!

13. Get your garnish options ready! You can garnish with chopped chillies & parsley and hopefully you made the Gremolata Sauce so you can take that out of the fridge ready to go!

CPSIA information can be obtained
at www.ICGtesting.com
Printed in the USA
LVHW020814280521
688664LV00004B/446